"Those who mind don't matter, and those who matter don't mind."
—Unknown

How many times does Buddy Bee appear inside this book, not including covers? (Answer is on copyright page.)

Jojo Giraffe's
BIG LAUGH

KIM LINETTE
illustrated by James Loram

Hmmm...

"Hmmm..." said Jojo Giraffe.
"What'cha doing?"
"Hiding," whispered Kali.

"HIDING?!" shouted Jojo. "Why would a fine human like you waste a beautiful afternoon hiding in a tree?"

"Shhhh! They'll hear you," warned Kali.
"Who?" whispered Jojo Giraffe.
"The other kids. They make fun of me for climbing trees, and they say I'm too short," said Kali, starting to cry.

"Hiding can be fun," said Jojo. "But crying? Not so much. I'd rather laugh!"

"Laugh?" asked Kali. "I don't see ANY reason to laugh, Ms. Giraffe."

"You can call me Jojo," said the giraffe. "And maybe things don't look funny YET, Ms. . . . ?"

"Kali," she replied.

"Well Kali, I want to share with you something that I think might make you feel better. It's called PERSPECTIVE—a new way of looking at things. With a new perspective, you'll see why things can often be funny instead of sad. Come with me!"

"Wow," said Kali. "Everything looks really different up here!"

"Yes, seeing the big view—the BIG PERSPECTIVE—is one of the great things about being a giraffe. And though you aren't a giraffe," giggled Jojo, "I CAN show you how to have a bigger, happier perspective and a bigger, happier laugh, too!

"See those young giraffes?" asked Jojo.

"Years ago, I was a young calf like them, except I wasn't very happy. Some of the giraffes made fun of me and said my spots looked weird because they were different. I felt sad and cried a lot."

"I'd be sad, too," said Kali.

"The worst part was that I BELIEVED the other giraffes," said Jojo, rolling her big eyes. "I BELIEVED my spots looked weird. I was so embarrassed about my spots that I ran home crying."

"That day, Mama Giraffe wiped my tears and taught me something very important," said Jojo. "Mama said, 'Little Jojo, whatever you do in life, don't take anything personally.'

"She said, 'When you take something personally, it means you think what someone else says or does is all about YOU. Wise giraffes know that just because someone says something about you, it doesn't mean it's true or that it's even about YOU. In fact, what others say actually tells a lot more about them!'

"And guess what?" asked Jojo. "Since that day, I saw how silly it was to take things personally. Stick with me and you'll see, too!"

"Ms. Ant, what do you think of me?" asked Jojo.

"Well, you seem nice enough," said the ant as she hurried along. "But I must say, giraffes stand around way too much. You really SHOULD be busier, like us ants. See all of these great ant hills we've built?"

"Hee, hee! Thank you for the input, Ms. Ant," giggled Jojo as the ant scurried off.

"Why do you laugh, Jojo Giraffe?" asked Kali. "Ms. Ant just said you aren't busy enough. Doesn't that make you feel bad about yourself?"

"Not at all," giggled Jojo. "Ms. Ant is just thinking like an ant. And while I think her perspective is interesting, I don't take it personally. I like how I spend my days.

"Can you imagine me . . .

"... ACTING LIKE AN ANT?!"

"Hello, Mr. Hippo," said Jojo, as they approached a pond. "When you look at me, what do you see?"

"Well," answered Mr. Hippo. "You seem like a pleasant giraffe. But I must say, I think your neck is WAY too long!"

"Thank you for the feedback, Mr. Hippo," chuckled Jojo.

"Why do you laugh?" asked Kali. "Doesn't it make you upset that Mr. Hippo doesn't like your neck?"

"No, Kali. Not at all. Mr. Hippo is just thinking like a hippo. I laugh because I know better. Can you imagine me . . ."

"... WITH A HIPPO NECK?!"

"Hee, hee! How would I eat the leaves off the tall trees? Now, I COULD choose to take what he said personally and feel bad about it. But I don't want to be a hippo. I'm proud of who I am. Thinking of myself with a hippo neck just makes me laugh," said Jojo.

"Kali, are you starting to see?" asked Jojo. "Whatever others say or do is from THEIR perspective. I learned long ago: there's no sense arguing with a hippo or ant or anyone else who doesn't really understand me. It's better to just listen politely, and then choose what *I* believe. That way I save my time and energy for things I love, like hanging around with folks who like me just the way I am."

"It's getting late, Kali. Should we talk to one more neighbor before we go back?"

"Yes!" said Kali. "But this time, can I ask the question?"

"Sure," nodded Jojo with her long giraffe neck.

"Mrs. Zebra," grinned Kali. "I'm curious, what do you think of me?"

"Well," said Mrs. Zebra looking closely at Kali. "You seem like a nice human. But I think you would be much more stylish if you had stripes like me!"

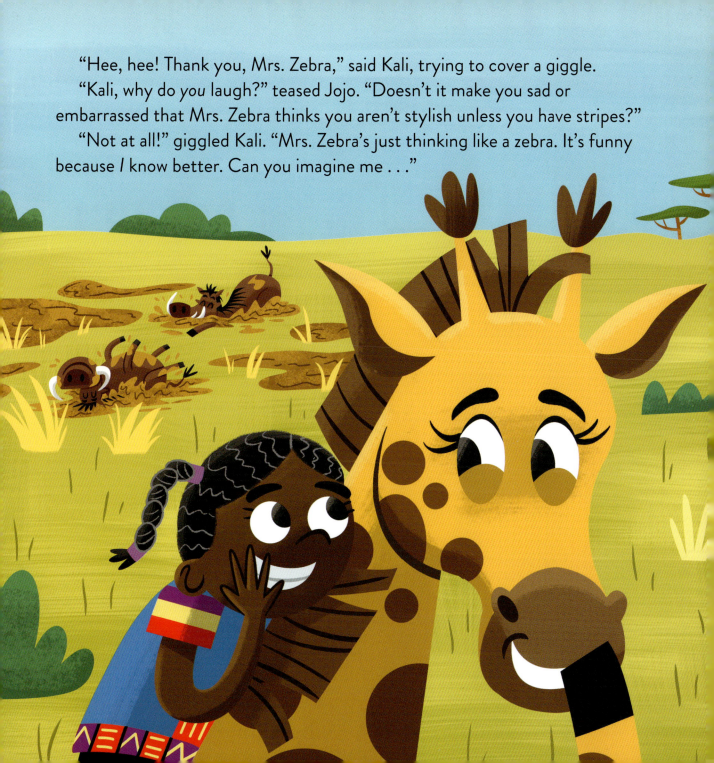

"Hee, hee! Thank you, Mrs. Zebra," said Kali, trying to cover a giggle.

"Kali, why do you laugh?" teased Jojo. "Doesn't it make you sad or embarrassed that Mrs. Zebra thinks you aren't stylish unless you have stripes?"

"Not at all!" giggled Kali. "Mrs. Zebra's just thinking like a zebra. It's funny because *I* know better. Can you imagine me . . ."

"... WITH ZEBRA STRIPES?!"

Kali and Jojo burst out laughing.
"Jojo Giraffe, you are right! I like my new perspective. I'm a lot happier when I don't take things personally. Except . . ."

"Except what, Kali?" asked Jojo Giraffe. "Why do you look so sad?"

"Well," said Kali, frowning. "I just started thinking—my friends aren't ants or hippos or zebras. They're people like me. Shouldn't I believe what THEY say about me?"

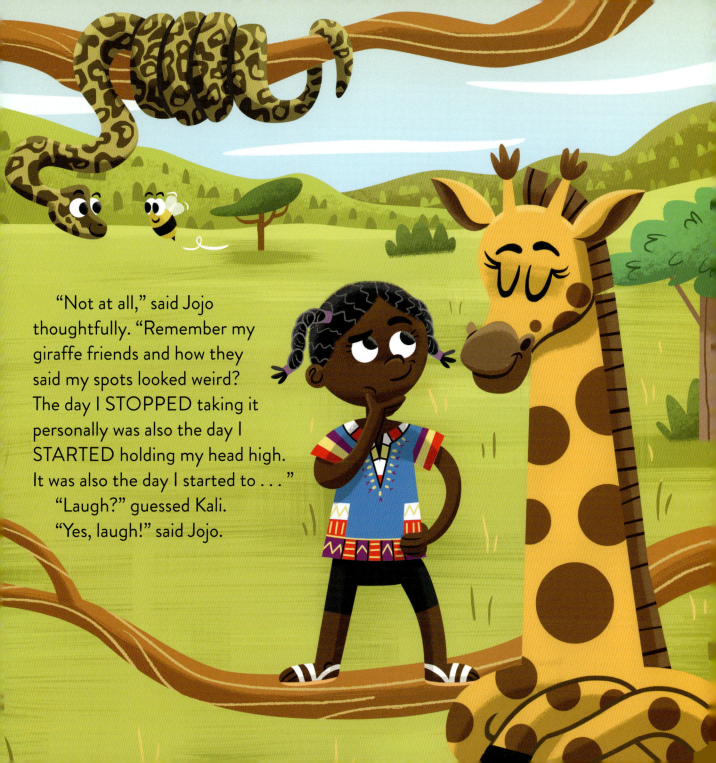

"Not at all," said Jojo thoughtfully. "Remember my giraffe friends and how they said my spots looked weird? The day I STOPPED taking it personally was also the day I STARTED holding my head high. It was also the day I started to . . ."

"Laugh?" guessed Kali.

"Yes, laugh!" said Jojo.

"Okay," said Kali. "Tell me, Jojo: why did you laugh THAT day?"

"I laughed," said Jojo, "because when I looked around, I noticed EVERY giraffe had different-looking spots. Ha! Did you know that no two giraffes will EVER have the exact same spots? I wasted so much time feeling sad because my spots were different, when all along no one had—or will ever have—the same spots!"

"And I realized that even if I COULD, I wouldn't WANT to be just like someone else. Our different spots make us interesting and unique," chuckled Jojo.

"That day, I also noticed something else VERY important. I noticed that grumpy giraffes, just like grumpy people, tend to say unkind things.

WOW, I DON'T LIKE YOUR SPOTS. THEY LOOK WEIRD!

"So, you see, others' opinions say a lot more about THEM and very little about YOU or ME. The truth is: human or giraffe, we're all different," proclaimed Jojo. "We all have things that are special about us.

"That day I stopped taking things personally and starting seeing the big perspective. That day, I also found my BIG laugh! Life's a lot more fun now!"

"I can see that, too!" said Kali with a smile. "I can see how many things in life are funny, instead of upsetting, now that *I* also have a bigger perspective."

"Exactly!" said Jojo.

"Hee hee," giggled Kali.

"I'm so glad you're laughing now! What's so funny?" asked Jojo.

"I'm thinking about when you found me up in the tree. Jojo, what if everyone took what *I* said personally? What if *I* said that everyone should like climbing trees?

"Can you imagine all of these animals . . .

"... TRYING TO CLIMB A TREE?!

"Jojo, thank you for sharing a new perspective! From now on, if kids start teasing me, I'm going to remember not to take it personally. Instead of feeling sad, I'm going to imagine you with me ..."

" . . . UP IN A TREE!
"FROM NOW ON, I'M GOING TO LAUGH!"

LET'S EXPLORE!

Share a time when someone teased you or said unkind things to you.
- How did you feel?
- Did you believe it was true?
- Did you take their words personally?
- What might have been going on inside the other person that made them say unkind things?
- What could you have done so you didn't take their words personally?

What great things could you do with the extra energy you would save by not taking anything personally?

FUN FACTS ABOUT GIRAFFES

1. Just as snowflakes or human fingerprints are unique, no two giraffes have the same spot pattern.
2. Baby giraffes, called "calves," average about 6 feet tall (1.8 m) when they are born. They can stand up just a half hour after birth. After just ten hours, they can run.
3. Giraffes spend most of their lives standing up . . . they even sleep standing up.
4. Young giraffes hang out in nursery groups until they are around five months old, resting and playing together while their mothers search for food.
5. Giraffe tongues are very long—so long that they can even clean their noses and ears with their tongues!

*For the children of this remarkable planet and for
those who nurture and care for them.*

*Special thanks to the village of Katzakalowa, Malawi.
Your enthusiasm for learning gives me a bigger perspective
and continues to inspire me. Zikomo!*
—K.L.

Buddy Bee appears 19 times in this book (not including the covers).

100% of profits from EQ Explorers books help nurture and empower underserved children. Kapalua Cove provides direct donations to charitable initiatives and donates books to orphanages, remote libraries, care centers, and more.

For additional reading and resources visit: EQExplorers.com

Jojo Giraffe's Big Laugh
All text and illustrations Copyright © 2019 by Kapalua Cove, LLC, Alpine, Utah

All rights reserved.

No part of this publication may be reproduced, stored in a retrieval system or transmitted in any form by any means, electronic, mechanical, photocopy, recording, or otherwise, without the prior permission of the publisher, except for the use of quotations in articles or reviews, or as provided by US copyright law.

For information, please contact: info@kapaluacove.com

Cover and Illustrations by James Loram, represented by Lemonade Illustration Agency

ISBN: 978-1-950062-02-7

Library of Congress Control Number: 2019948307

Printed in Malaysia

First Edition

1 3 5 7 9 10 8 6 4 2

End notes from front flap:
1. http://adultdevelopment.wix.com/harvardstudy; Travis Bradbury and Jean Greaves, *Emotional Intelligence 2.0*, (San Diego: Talent Smart, 2009).
2. Dr. John Gottman, *Raising an Emotionally Intelligent Child* (New York: Fireside Books, 1998).